# The Funny Guide to Pickleball

Excuses, Obsessions,
and the Hilarious Truth about Pickleball Players

**Ricky Woods**

Copyright © 2025 Ricky Woods

Published by: Bemberton Ltd

All rights reserved. No part of this book or any portion thereof may be reproduced in any form by any electronic or mechanical means, without permission in writing from the publisher, except for the use of brief quotes in a book review.

The publisher accepts no legal responsibility for any action taken by the reader, including but not limited to financial losses or damages, both directly or indirectly incurred as a result of the content in this book.

ISBN: 978-1-918027-09-9

Disclaimer: The information in this book is general and designed to be for information only. While every effort has been made to ensure it is wholly accurate and complete, it is for general information only. It is not intended, nor should it be taken as professional advice. The author gives no warranties or undertakings whatsoever concerning the content. The reader accepts that the author is not responsible for any action, including but not limited to losses both directly or indirectly incurred by the reader as a result of the content in this book

View all our books at **bemberton.com**

# CONTENTS

| | |
|---|---|
| 5 | Introduction |
| 9 | What the Hell Is Pickleball? |
| 17 | Fine, I'll Try It — but Only Once |
| 25 | Buying the Paddle of Shame |
| 33 | Dink or Die |
| 41 | Joining the League of Mid-Lifers |
| 49 | The Conversion Is Complete |
| 57 | Pickleball Injuries. Wait, Pickleball Injuries?!? |
| 65 | Court Drama and Paddle Politics |
| 71 | Chapter Letting Your Pickleball Freak Flag Fly |
| 79 | Becoming a Lifer |
| 87 | Conclusion |

# INTRODUCTION

Pickleball was never supposed to be a part of your life.

In fact, you didn't even know what it was, and you were perfectly happy that way.

You already had a good life. You weren't searching, or seeking, or wandering. You were content, happy, and healthy. Life was good, and no dramatic, revolutionary change was needed to get you back on track.

But it happened anyway.

This is not a book about pickleball. Well, not in the traditional sense.

We aren't going to go over the rules or offer swing advice or strategy tips. There are plenty of those books available, of course, but that's not what you'll find here.

Rather, this is more of a story about what happens when pickleball grabs you around the ankles and won't let go. It's a journey from start to finish, from complete beginner to total lifer.

# A COMMON AFFLICTION

As you read this book, you'll likely find the story sounds pretty familiar.

In some parts, it might sound a little *too* familiar.

However, you can take solace in the fact that you are not alone in this journey. Not even close.

Pickleball has swept like a tidal wave across the United States in recent years. It's popping up everywhere you look.

To an outsider, it's hard to see what all the fuss is about.

To an insider, it's hard to remember what life was like before owning a paddle and a pair of court shoes.

In virtually every city across the country, if you listen hard enough on a Saturday morning, you can hear the "dink, dink, dink" of a pickleball off in the distance.

It's become the suburban version of the rooster crowing at sunrise.

# DON'T THINK YOU ARE IMMUNE

It's possible that you are reading this book while remaining on the outside. You haven't yet started to play pickleball. You think you are safe. How cute.

No one is safe from the insidious nature of this game. As you'll see in the chapters that follow, it starts innocently enough.

You don't set out to start playing pickleball. You aren't even interested, and there are plenty of other things that keep you busy in life.

If you read the chapters that follow and think that nothing like this will ever happen to you, be careful with that confidence. Soon enough, you may find yourself dressed head-to-toe in moisture-wicking fabrics as you retape the handle of your paddle for the third time in a week.

Life comes at you fast.

# WHAT THE HELL IS PICKLEBALL?                    1

**"Pickleball is not a sport. It's a midlife crisis with a paddle."**

At some point, you saw it. And, let's be honest, you didn't think much of it.

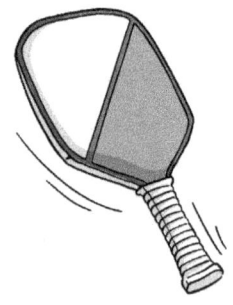

A weird game. On a tiny court. With adults smacking a plastic ball like they were playing tennis at a preschool.

You stared. You frowned. You moved on.

Sure, it looked ridiculous — half-sized courts, paddles that seemed like someone left a tennis racket in the dryer too long, and a ball that could've come from a child's toy bin. It wasn't worth your time or curiosity. You had better things to do. Real sports to play. A dog to walk. Maybe a proper game of tennis. Definitely not whatever that was. Whatever this was, it didn't matter. Life moved on.

Until it didn't.

Maybe it was another walk in the park. Maybe your kids spotted it from the car and started laughing. "Why are grown-ups playing on a baby tennis court?" they asked, giggling.

This time, something sticks. You need to know. Why is this everywhere? Why are so many people into it? Did tennis get canceled? Is this some kind of rehab activity for people afraid of cardio? The questions build. The curiosity festers.

You need answers. So you do what you always do in moments of confusion and existential crisis. You Google it.

## THE CONFUSION DEEPENS

Normally, Google clears things up fast. Type half a question, and boom — you get the answer.

How much does a giraffe weigh? Easy. (Around 2,600 pounds, if you're curious.)

How far away is the sun? 93 million miles. Obviously.

But this is trickier. What do you even type?

"Mini tennis game with plastic ball?"

"Old people tennis with paddles?"

"Weird sport everyone at the park is playing and won't shut up about?"

Eventually, you get your answer.

**Pickleball.**

Wait, what? This already looked like a dumb sport, but it has a name that sounds like something you'd eat at the fair. Pickel. Ball. Seriously?

Once you stop laughing at the name and land on the Wikipedia page, you realize pickleball isn't new at all. It's been around since the '60s — a long-time favorite of bored PE teachers and gym-class awkwardness. So if it's not new, why is it suddenly everywhere? You're not sure, but deep down, you suspect millennials are to blame.

## A COMPLETE DISMISSAL

You tumble down the pickleball rabbit hole — videos, articles, diagrams — and still come up empty. You've seen how it's played. You've read the hype about it being "the sport of the masses." And yet...it all feels weirdly off.

But even in your confusion, one thing is crystal clear:

**You are never playing this game.**

Not today. Not ever.

You have zero interest in pickleball. The name alone disqualifies it. And you wouldn't be caught dead holding one of those paddles — or rackets, or bats, or whatever the hell they're called.

You've got better things to do with your time.

Like golf.

Sure, your clubs have been gathering dust in the garage for years, but you're definitely getting back out there again. Soon.

Or that mountain bike with the flat tire and the rusted chain. Yeah. You're about to relaunch your biking career and a new era of hardcore trail riding. Any day now. Anyone ever get that kind of adrenaline rush from playing pickleball? Didn't think so.

Your mental list keeps growing — fishing, running, weightlifting, axe throwing, anything. Literally anything is a better use of your time.

Pickleball isn't on the list.

And it never will be.

## GROWING ANNOYANCE WITH THE TREND

Something about this so-called sport starts to fester.

You're not interested in playing — obviously — but you can't stop thinking about it. Why is everyone suddenly obsessed?

Why are matches on TV? Why are celebrities posing with paddles like it's the new Pilates?

Why, why, why?

And now...you're a little angry. Not just at the sport, but at the people who play it. They seem so smug. So self-satisfied. Don't they realize it's easy? Anyone can tap a plastic ball over a waist-high net. Adults getting a thrill from mastering a kid's game? Please. Grow up.

Even the sound is irritating.

You walk past a few doubles games and complain loudly — to no one in particular — about how aggravating it is. It's not the clean thwack of a tennis racket. It's more like someone knocking on a hollow door. Repeatedly. At random intervals. Forever.

Do these people ever stop? Can't a sane person walk by without being audibly assaulted by the pop-pop-pop of middle-aged ambition?

Worse, you start bringing up pickleball in conversations. Unprovoked.

No one else is talking about it — hell, no one's even talking about sports — but you find a way. Every time. And if someone dares say something positive? Boom. You unload—a full takedown of why it's dumb, pointless, and overrated.

It doesn't land well.

You start losing people. But that's fine. You've accepted your new role: full-time anti-pickleball crusader.

And you're not backing down.

## YOU ALREADY KNOW SOME OF THESE NUTS

The more you bring up pickleball—usually uninvited—the more inevitable it becomes: You're going to run into someone who actually plays.

It's just math. Millions of people are now obsessed, so odds are, a few have infiltrated your life.

At first, most players just smile awkwardly and say nothing. People hate confrontation, so they nod along as you rant and pretend they've never set foot on a court.

But not everyone plays nice.

Sooner or later, someone breaks. They speak up. And with alarming sincerity, they say it:

"I love pickleball."

Wait — what? **Them?**

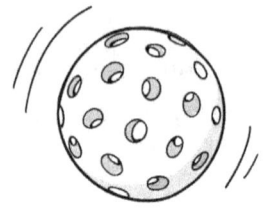

This is someone you like. Or at least, used to. Someone with decent taste. Someone you'd invite to dinner. And now here they are, proudly declaring their love for the game you've built your personality around hating.

It rattles you.

Not because you're rethinking pickleball. No — your opinion on that is rock solid. What shifts is your view of them.

They can't actually think it's fun. They must be pretending. Giving in to peer pressure. Joining the cult — a bunch of sweaty, paddle-wielding sheep.

You shake your head in disbelief, and you double down. Because if there's one thing you still know for certain — etched deep into your soul — it's this:

You are never playing pickleball.

Nope.
Never.
**Not gonna happen.**

# FINE, I'LL TRY IT— BUT ONLY ONCE

# 2

By now, your circle of friends and family is familiar with your growing disdain for the popular sport. They don't dare talk about it in your presence, let alone invite you out for a game.

But then, something unexpected happens. You do get invited, and for some reason — social pressure, guilt, curiosity — you feel like you have to say yes. Maybe it's someone you know professionally, and you don't want to be rude. Maybe it's a friend you haven't seen in a while.

Suddenly, you find yourself staring blankly, trying to think of what to say. Do you decline and risk the social — or professional — fallout? Or do you break with your personal ethos against all things paddle and agree to join the match?

It might not be an existential crisis, but it's close.

## THE DREADED YES

You barely make an audible sound. The person who invited you to play pickleball is still staring, waiting for an answer. Under the gun, you freeze up, panic a bit, and feel like you have to say something. Anything.

It comes out as a "Yes."

They don't hear you, of course. Prodded again, you say it louder. They smile and promise to send more details about the date and time.

As your newfound pickleball buddy strolls away, you stand still, in silent disbelief. How did this happen? You're going to play pickleball? You *hate* pickleball!

Soon after, you start rationalizing. It's okay. You aren't going to become a pickleball player. You're just helping out a friend — being a good person. It's not like one outing is going to destine you to a life of dinking the ball back and forth over that dumb little net. Right? Right.

## PRE-GAME PANIC

The day of the match arrives. It's nothing serious, of course — just a casual doubles game among friends. You don't own any pickleball gear, but your friend promises they have everything you'll need. Just dress appropriately and you'll be all set.

But what's appropriate for pickleball? How do you dress as an adult playing a game that appears to be designed for kids?

At first, you dress like you're going to the gym. But that feels too casual. Then you switch it up and dress like you're playing golf. But that's too formal, and you can't really move around freely.

After a few costume changes, you go back to gym clothes and decide that you don't care what anyone thinks. This is still a dumb game, after all.

On the drive to the court, the nerves set in. Despite not caring about this game, you're surprisingly anxious. What if you're really bad at pickleball?

Even worse, what if you're really good?

You start thinking about how hard to try. It feels like you should give an honest effort, but sprinting around the court would show too much commitment.

Your goal is to land somewhere in the middle. As you pull into the parking lot, you decide to do just enough to help your partner a little bit — but no more.

With a deep breath, you lock the car and walk to the court. The moment is here, and it's sure to be a colossal waste of time.

# FIRST IMPRESSIONS

Somehow, the court is smaller than you thought it would be. It's always looked small from a distance, but now that you're standing on it, the dimensions are comical. This is what all the fuss is about?

Next, someone hands you a paddle. You hold it for the first time, although not enthusiastically. It's tiny like the court, but heavier than it looks. The ball feels like a toy you'd give to a toddler.

So far, your opinions have been justified. This all looks pretty stupid. And then it gets worse. The other players start to explain the rules, including what all of these lines mean. You know how tennis works, but this is different. For some reason, the area by the net is called the "kitchen," and you can't go in there. Except when you can. Someone must have written these rules while drunk.

Who cares? You'll just hit the ball back and forth for a while and move on. If these dorks want to worry about the rules, that's their problem.

# THE MID-MATCH REVELATION

At the start of the game, you're very self-conscious. Not only are you on guard about your abilities, but you're also careful not to be seen having too much fun.

What you're doing can best be described as "going through the motions."

After a while, however, something changes. You start moving without thinking. You're flowing with the game.

At one point, you hit a great shot that splits your opponents and lands for a winner. You quickly smile before trying to hide your excitement.

You and your partner even manage to win a game. Sure, you lost the others, but that one win was genuinely fun. The teamwork felt good, and it was a thrill to perform under pressure.

There was another thought that lingered during the match: You might be good at this.

This was your first time playing, and did you see some of those shots? You hit several winners! With a bit of work on your serve and a better understanding of strategy, that other team wouldn't have stood a chance.

# A CONFLICTED CAR RIDE HOME

So, it's over. You've played your first pickleball match and lived to tell about it.

The thing is, you aren't going to tell anyone — because you actually liked it. All those nasty things you said about the game didn't hold up. It's not a waste of time. It's not just for kids. And sure, the noise of the ball hitting the paddle is annoying, but you didn't even notice it by the end.

You were having too much fun.

All of this makes for a strange ride home. What do you feel? What are you *supposed* to feel? And more importantly, how can you get back onto a pickleball court without anyone knowing?

You might not fully know it yet, but the pickleball train has officially left the station — and it doesn't have any brakes.

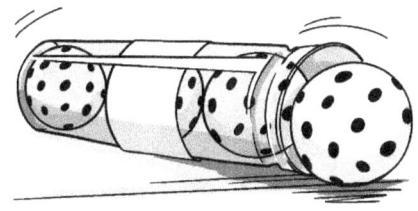

# BUYING THE
# PADDLE OF SHAME

# 3

The reality of the situation is this:

You are now a pickleball player. You might not have seen that coming, but as soon as you reluctantly accepted that first invite, this future was assured.

Now, you're facing an unexpected milestone. You need to buy some gear. Specifically, you need a paddle.

This is a turning point, because once there's a pickleball paddle in your closet — or in your trunk — the denials are harder to maintain. Borrowing a paddle is one thing. It's easy to pass that off as being helpful or social. But buying one? That's commitment.

This is who you are now.

## GOING DOWN THE RESEARCH SPIRAL

It starts innocently enough. You Google "best pickleball paddle for beginners" and start browsing.

Three hours later, you're wondering what happened to your Saturday afternoon. Did your spouse and kids leave the house? Who knows, and who cares.

There's just so much to learn — starting with the brand names, which are somehow as odd as the sport itself.

JOOLA. Selkirk. Onix. It's like someone spun a wheel of syllables and called it a business.

Eventually, you stumble across an online quiz that promises to match you with the perfect paddle. It asks a few vague questions, then spits out your Pickleball Persona.

You are a "Strategic Technician."

That sounds pretty good. So what if you've only played a few games and barely understand the rules? You're owning the title, and you're using it to justify what happens next.

## WINDOW SHOPPING— WITH CREDIT CARD IN HAND

Even now, with a few games played and hours of research under your belt, you still tell yourself you're not fully committed. It feels like this hobby could go either way. Maybe you'll get a golf invite and turn back.

One day after work, you stop by a sporting goods store — just to look, not to buy. You just want to hold a few paddles and get a feel for them. Your credit card is in your pocket, but you're definitely not using it today.

While you're browsing, a cheerful salesperson walks over. "How often do you play? Are you in any leagues? What kind of player are you?"

You answer the first two honestly enough. "Not very often" and "definitely not."

But the third one? That one gets you. Despite your better judgment, your eyes light up as you reply: "I'm a Strategic Technician."

Just like that, the wheels are set in motion. The salesperson smiles. They've found their mark.

"This paddle is great for beginners, but you look a little more advanced than that. Check this one out. Sure, it costs a bit more, but the control you get is worth every penny. As a technician, you'll love the way it responds."

You nod along like you understand everything they're saying. You don't, but it doesn't matter.

28

# THE FIRST PURCHASE

You can hardly believe it as your credit card hits the counter. Are you really doing this? Buying a paddle?

Yes. Yes, you are.

In truth, you're excited. Now that the charade is over, you're starting to imagine your future on the court. Winning matches. Making friends. Owning your spot at the net.

And there's a bonus revelation — pickleball is relatively affordable. For under $100, you can get a solid paddle. Even the high-end models are a fraction of what you'd pay for one golf club.

And golf requires 14!

There's a surprising spring in your step as you leave the store. Do you toss the paddle in the trunk? No. It rides in the passenger seat.

# WHAT ELSE DO YOU NEED?

Of course, the paddle is just the beginning. You start thinking about the gear other players have. What are they bringing to the court that you're not?

Apparel, for starters. You didn't feel quite right in your outfit during that first game. You remember spotting some sleek shirts and shorts at the store. Adding a couple of those would boost your confidence — and probably make you play better, too.

You also need balls. You can't keep showing up empty-handed. Plus, you want to practice alone — maybe in the garage, just hitting against the wall when no one's watching.

And shoes. You need proper court shoes with non-marking soles. Your current pair of tennis shoes just doesn't feel stable when you move laterally.

# A LOOK IN THE MIRROR

Eventually, all the gear shows up — the outfits, the balls, the accessories. It builds slowly at first, and then all at once.

One day, you're getting ready for a game and catch a glimpse of yourself in the mirror.

What. The. Hell.

You barely recognize yourself. Paddle bag slung over your shoulder. Branded pickleball hat. Deep tan lines across your calves. Wristbands. Matching socks.

You're a walking, talking billboard for the game you used to mock.

## A HOBBY COMING TO LIFE

And yet...

You haven't felt this excited about something in a while. Buying the gear has only added fuel to the fire. Where you once tried to downplay your interest, you now embrace it. You're not just playing pickleball. You're a pickleballer.

You don't know exactly where this is going, but one thing is clear: You're all in.

And you love it.

# DINK OR DIE

**4**

33

A short time ago, you were baffled by how much time people spent playing pickleball. It seemed ridiculous.

Now? The only thing that seems ridiculous is the fact that some people don't play. What are they thinking?

You are head over heels in love. Your personal and professional life revolves around your pickleball schedule. Far more thought goes into picking a pickleball partner than a romantic mate.

The stakes are much higher on the court, after all.

## SIGNS OF OBSESSIVE PICKLEBALL BEHAVIOR

Pickleball has started to change your behavior in a number of different ways. You might not notice it, but those around you sure do.

The first major shift is your schedule. Before, you might have fit in a hobby or some exercise when the opportunity came up. If it didn't fit in, no big deal. You'd do something the next weekend.

Now, it's pickleball first. No matter what, you are getting in a match. And some practice. And a workout in the gym.

You are acting like a professional athlete who also has to fit in a full-time job and family duties.

Does it make sense? No, not really. But "sense" is out the window at this point.

When you receive invitations to events, they are filtered first through your pickleball schedule. Attend a birthday party? That's a maybe. Work overtime on a weekend for your job? Only if it's going to rain.

There are also the subtle movements that sneak into your daily life. While waiting in line at the grocery store, you practice your serve technique. Sitting on the sidelines at your kid's soccer game becomes the perfect time to master your footwork.

You don't care if people see you exhibiting these odd behaviors. In fact, you prefer it. If a question comes up, it gives you the opportunity to say three words that suddenly fill you with pride: "I'm a pickleballer."

Referring to yourself as "a pickleballer" is something you do without a hint of self-consciousness or shame. You are as proud as could be.

Wearing your court shoes in regular, everyday settings is another sign that you are obsessed. No, you don't have a match scheduled for today, but hey, you never know. Might as well lace 'em up and be ready, just in case.

## LETTING THE LINGO SLIP

As if "pickleballer" wasn't a bad enough addition to your vocabulary, there is more. So much more.

On the court, there is a certain lingo that players use amongst themselves — which is fair enough. Every sport has a language of its own.

But that language should stay on the court. It has no business in day-to-day life. And it certainly makes no sense to people who don't claim membership in the Cult of the Paddle.

When someone gets a little too into your business at work, you might tell them to "stay out of your kitchen." And you are serious, as if that makes any sense at all to a normal person.

In a disagreement with your spouse, you might state that you would like them to "dink more and drive less."

In your mind, that means they should be gentle and not so aggressive. In their mind, however, they have no idea what the hell you are talking about.

And so it goes. Each new phrase you pick up on the court will soon be used in real life. Every once in a while, you'll use your lingo in the presence of another player, and they'll love it. Otherwise, people will just look at you like you have two heads.

## WORKING ON YOUR PICKLEBALL PHD

As much as you've fallen for pickleball, you still have a lot to learn.

This game is more complicated than it looks from the outside. Points move fast, and your opponents always seem to be one step ahead.

So, now it's time to study. Constantly. Like every other scholar of the 21st century, you start your studies in the obvious place: YouTube.

You soon find yourself following accounts called "Coach Pickle" or "Dink Wizard."

You subscribe to every pickleball channel you can find and consume hours of content each day. From slow-motion breakdowns of professional matches to technical explanations of the best way to hit a volley, you are there for it all.

Written instruction falls into your hands, as well. You never were much of a reader before, but you're now burning the midnight oil to pick up every last tip you can find on pickleball game theory. No advantage is too small when it comes to gaining an edge on the competition.

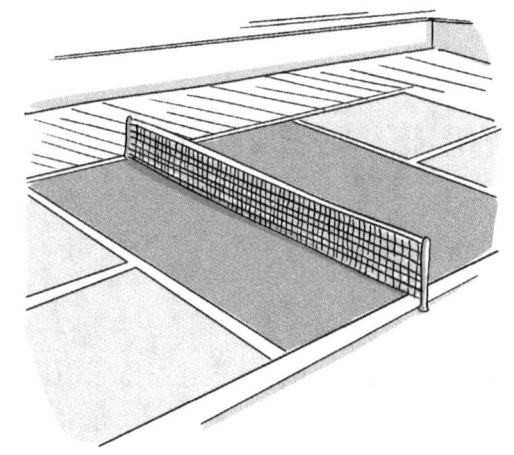

As your knowledge grows, so does your confidence in sharing it with everyone. Literally everyone. From co-workers to fast food workers to your children and beyond, no one is safe.

You'll quickly pull out your phone at a moment's notice and say something like "Come here and watch how this game point was strategically constructed."

Did anyone ask? Not at all. Is that going to stop you? No chance.

# SURVIVING A DAY OFF

You went your entire life without playing pickleball. It never occurred to you to think about having a "day off" from this sport, because every day was a day off.

Suddenly, and without warning, not playing pickleball for a day seems like punishment. It's like fasting. You might be able to make it through, but it sure feels like you are going to die.

As hard as you fight it, however, a day off is needed.

You have played for six days in a row. At first, your Apple Watch was congratulating you on all of this newfound activity. Now it is sending you warnings. Slow down buddy, something is going to blow.

With creaking knees and a sore shoulder, you decide to take Sunday off. Do something else. Get away from the game.

It doesn't go well. Others in your pickleball group chat are playing. You keep seeing the messages. You are dying to get in a game.

By noon, you are wearing your pickleball clothes. Not to play, just to be comfortable. But that doesn't scratch the itch. You are staring at your paddle bag in the corner, and it's begging you to pick it up and head to the park.

By three, you are warming up and waiting for your turn to jump in for a game. You are at the park, lurking around courts where you know no one at all.

Whether out of kindness or pity, the strangers let you play. Your craving has been satisfied.

You didn't get your day off, and your joints are worse than ever, but hey — at least you'll be able to sleep tonight.

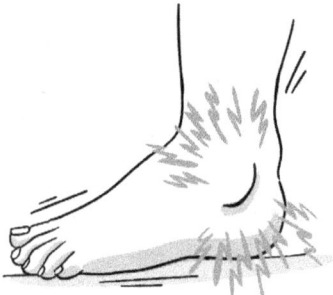

# BUY A TICKET, TAKE THE RIDE

When you first started to dip your toe into the shallow end of the pickleball pond, it felt wrong. It was disingenuous and counter to your previous opinions on the sport.

Now, you can't even see the shallow end. You are in the deep end, swimming with the sharks, and would have it no other way.

At this point, if anyone tried to take your paddle away, they'd have to pry it out of your sweaty, blistered, and somewhat sunburned fingers.

# JOINING THE LEAGUE OF MID-LIFERS

# 5

Recreational pickleball is fine. Playing pick-up matches with a few friends — or whoever is around at the local court — is what led you down this rabbit hole in the first place.

But it's not enough anymore. What you need is competition — to face other players who are just as paddle-obsessed as you are. It's time for a league.

Add this to the list of steps you never imagined you'd take. Pickleball leagues are for people with nothing better to do. They have a childish need to prove their superiority in this silly, made-up little game.

And they are now your people. You know that joining a pickleball league — or a few leagues — might signal the arrival of a mid-life crisis. But who cares? Bring it on.

## NAVIGATING THE RATING SYSTEM

Pickleball leagues come in all shapes and sizes, but they all have one thing in common — a spot on the entry form for your rating.

You've probably heard about ratings, but maybe you've never had one of your own. You aren't entirely sure what they mean, or how they work.

Nevertheless, you have to put something in that field. Anything. There's nothing official here — you just decide what your rating is, and that's what it is.

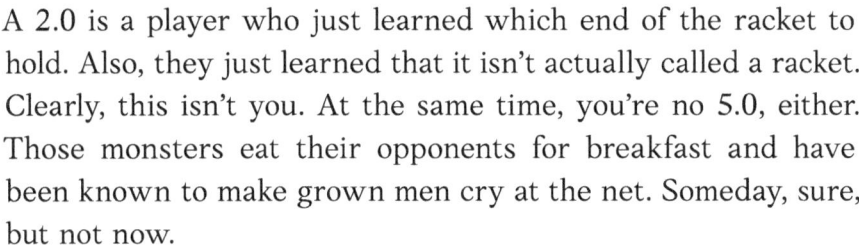

After a quick web search and some Reddit browsing, you learn that the scale runs from 2.0 to 5.0 — which is a dumb range for a scale. What kind of scale works like that? Even the notoriously arbitrary scale of Imperial units makes more sense than pickleball ratings.

A 2.0 is a player who just learned which end of the racket to hold. Also, they just learned that it isn't actually called a racket. Clearly, this isn't you. At the same time, you're no 5.0, either. Those monsters eat their opponents for breakfast and have been known to make grown men cry at the net. Someday, sure, but not now.

After much back and forth, you go with 3.5. Right in the middle. Not showing off, not falling behind.

Little did you know, damn near everyone in the league calls themselves a 3.5. Going with 3.0 would have allowed you to ease into things and taken a little pressure off.

But no longer. With a self-proclaimed 3.5 to your name, you'll be diving right in and hoping for the best.

# SWALLOWING YOUR NERVES

The rational side of your brain is telling you not to be nervous. It's ridiculous to be nervous about your first league match. It's just pickleball. You've played hundreds of matches by now, even if they were casual. And who cares if you lose? There's nothing on the line, anyway.

But it doesn't help. You are a bundle of nerves in the days leading up to the match. Sleep is hard to come by, and your family notices that you are distracted.

To deal with the nerves, you go into planning mode. You pick the right paddle for the court conditions. Your outfit is laid out days in advance. Checking the weather forecast begins to feel like a bodily function.

Despite time slowing to a crawl, matchday finally arrives. You arrive at the courts before anyone else, and the wait feels endless. Other players start to show up and you make nervous chatter in an attempt to calm down.

That doesn't work either. When it's time to hit the court for warm-ups, you can feel the paddle slipping around in your sweaty palm. This is going to be interesting.

# THE GLORY AND THE AGONY

Somehow, with the nerves flowing, you manage to win the first point of your league career.

Sure, it was an unforced error by the other team, but whatever. You'll take it.

That turns out to be the highlight of the game. It's a bloodbath. You make plenty of mistakes, and your partner isn't perfect, either. It seems the other team is a little more 3.5-ish than you are.

Final score, 11–2. Ouch.

Something weird happens along the way in that first game, however. You realize that even losing is fun. You start to see where you need to get better. The pressure of a formal match brings out weaknesses in your game that you didn't know existed.

You also notice that the people in the league are just like you. It's like looking in the mirror. They love to compete. They want to get better. They love pickleball down to the core.

And you can't shake the feeling of winning those points. You only won two, of course, but those moments of glory are burned in your brain.

Competitive pickleball is proving to be a drug, and you've just had your first high.

## TENSION AND TRASH TALK

It doesn't take long for league night to show its true colors. It's not all fun and games. And it's not all friendly.

These people like to talk some trash!

Knowing you are new, they take it easy at first. But a few of them can't help themselves.

"Nice shot—didn't think you had that one in the bag."

"Did you find your paddle in a thrift shop or by the side of the highway?"

"This next smash is going to leave 'Franklin' printed on your forehead."

The competitive fire only makes things more exciting. As the talk heats up, you feel more and more motivated to pull through and win some games. It feels great to win a heated point, and it feels even better to throw a bit of trash talk back over the net.

# GETTING AHEAD OF YOURSELF

As the league season plays out, you and your partner aren't at the bottom of the standings. You aren't at the top, either. But hey, staying out of last place is something to celebrate.

Not only do you celebrate, but you start to look ahead. If you've done this well in your rookie season, what could be next? Is the league championship within reach next year? If you win that trophy, will you move up to 4.0? Are there any harder leagues in your city that you could enter?

None of this is particularly rational or reasonable, but you can't help it. Your showers are spent practicing speeches to give to the crowd after you win a big league match. The pickleball world is soon to be your oyster.

All of this premature excitement is temporarily derailed by a rough defeat in the last match of the season. Two retirees with braces on every joint completely dismantle you and your partner. They don't say a single word the whole game, yet somehow knew each other's every move. It's a comprehensive beating from start to finish.

No matter. You see big things ahead in your pickleball future, and a few losses along the way aren't going to snuff out that candle.

# THE CONVERSION IS COMPLETE

# 6

Once upon a time, you had a balanced life. It wasn't that long ago.

Come to think of it, it was right before you picked up a pickleball paddle for the first time. You did a variety of things after work and on weekends, spent time with your family, and always got plenty of rest. It was lovely.

But those days are gone. You have now been completely consumed by pickleball, and it's hard to imagine life any other way.

Would a balanced life be healthier? Sure, probably. But do you care? Not at all. Whatever the future holds, they'll have to pry your carbon fiber paddle from your cold, lifeless fingers.

## SCHEDULING LIFE AROUND THE COURT

You can tell how serious a pickleball player is by the kind of calendar they keep.

Someone who has this hobby under control will simply add a few pickleball dates to their regular calendar. They might have a weekly league match, along with the occasional casual game. Those dates and times live on the same calendar

as everything else — doctor's appointments, family dinners, vacations, etc.

That's not how your calendar works at all. In fact, you don't have a single calendar. You have two.

There's a calendar for all of your pickleball-related activities, and then there's the other calendar. Truth be told, you don't look at that other calendar much anymore, and you see the items on it mainly as an inconvenience.

To anyone else, your pickleball calendar would look incredibly busy. Monday is open play night at your local courts. Tuesday is league night — and so is Thursday. You mark Wednesday as "rest," but that rarely happens.

Most Saturdays are filled with tournaments, which means Friday nights are spent preparing or traveling.

When someone asks if you're available for an event, or even a work meeting, you check your pickleball calendar first. Even if a day is technically open, it might be off-limits if there's an important match coming up. You've got to be fresh.

# PICKLEBALL IN THE OFFICE

Sadly, you are not a professional pickleball player. Not yet, anyway.

That means you still need to maintain employment, even if it gets in the way of your many paddle-related dreams. Of course, you always maintain professional standards and never bring your pickleball life into the office.

Well, that's how it started, at least. Early on, you didn't talk about pickleball much at work, unless it came up at lunch when coworkers were talking about their matches. Those conversations were fair game — but otherwise, work was work and play was play.

Inevitably, however, pickleball began to creep in. At first, it was minor. Maybe you forgot to change out of your court shoes before a client meeting. A little embarrassing, but not a big deal.

But then it gets worse. Soon enough, you're comparing business strategy to pickleball tactics.

During a planning session, you blurt out something like: "We need to slow things down, reset the point, and stop letting them pull us up into the kitchen."

To you, it makes perfect sense. To everyone else, it sounds like you've completely lost it.

No one laughs. No one even knows what to say. Eventually, someone changes the subject and pretends it didn't happen.

You are undeterred.

The pickleball references keep coming. You start wearing match day gear in professional settings. Colleagues begin to recognize the logos on your shirts. They ask fewer questions now. They've accepted who you are.

Are you going to lose your job over this obsession? Probably not. But if you do, that's just more time to train.

## INVADING THE HOME FRONT

Just as pickleball has infiltrated your work life, it's also taken over at home. You are the only person in your house who plays, yet you talk about it constantly.

When meeting new people, you introduce your spouse as your "doubles partner in training." Everyone laughs, except your spouse, who will have things to say about this on the way home.

At one point, the family gets a new dog. The kids are excited to name it something fun. You insist on naming it after your old doubles partner. They didn't die — they just pulled a hamstring and will be out for the season.

Like every obsessed pickleball player, there is one room in the house you now can't handle: the kitchen.

The jokes practically write themselves. Every time someone enters, whether to make breakfast or get a drink of water, you can't help yourself:

"Careful, you can't volley in there!"

"Did the ball bounce first?"

"Watch out, I'm going to lob you!"

At first, you got courtesy laughs. Now, just silence. Everyone is tired of the jokes. They've decided the best course of action, as when dealing with a toddler mid-meltdown, is to ignore you and move on.

# HITTING THE ROAD

With the home front getting chilly, there's only one solution: Hit the road.

Have you run out of worthy opponents in your city? Of course not. You didn't even finish in the top three in your league. But still.

Soon, the van is packed and you're driving eight hours through the night for a Saturday morning tournament in a converted warehouse. Living the dream.

These tournaments give you a taste of what it's like to be a professional athlete. Sure, you're staying in a Super 8 and surviving on free bagels and granola bars, but the vibe is there.

You hover around the bracket board, waiting to see if your rivals dropped a set. Watching scores go up and down like stock prices.

And somehow, despite having driven hundreds of miles to play a child's game with strangers, you've never felt more at home. This is where you belong. You are pickleball.

# PICKLEBALL INJURIES. WAIT, PICKLEBALL INJURIES?!? 7

One of the big selling points for pickleball is how much easier it is on your body than tennis.

Anyone who's played tennis knows it's a brutal sport. The constant running and changing directions wear out your joints almost immediately. Only the fittest of the fit can stay on a tennis court for a full match and still walk into the office the next day.

By opting for pickleball as your hobby (obsession) of choice, you get to avoid those risks. You can take to the court, have your fun, and leave no worse for wear.

Right? Not necessarily.

## THE FIRST INJURY: A BADGE OF HONOR

It's nearly impossible to get injured in your first few pickleball matches. You aren't moving fast enough for anything to stretch, strain, or tear. At most, you'll come away with a mild blister on your paddle hand, and that'll be it.

Soon enough, though, the game speeds up. You start to care more.

There's no way you're letting that guy beat you down the line with a winner.

So, you push yourself to your athletic limits. They might be modest limits, but they're limits all the same. A sprint here, a reach there — even the occasional dive. You're now putting your body on the line for a game you mocked not that long ago.

Then, one morning, you wake up with a weird pain. You don't think much of it and go about your day.

But it's still there the next morning. You doubt it's from pickleball. Probably just from all those stairs at the office. You'll take the elevator for a few days until it clears up.

It doesn't clear up. The pain persists — and it's particularly bad on the court.

And suddenly, it hits you: This is a **pickleball injury**.

You're mildly frustrated...but mostly you're proud. This is a milestone. You can hardly wait for your doctor's appointment, just so you can say the words out loud. "I got hurt playing pickleball."

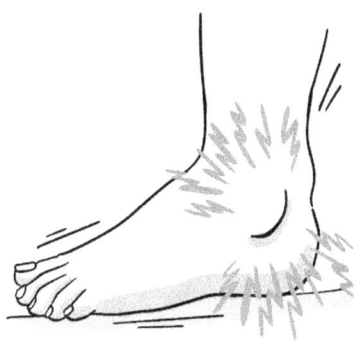

That just sounds so damn cool.

# THE STAGES OF PICKLEBALL INJURY

The cool factor wears off quickly. That first injury feels like entry into a club. The next ones? Not so fun. They threaten to take away the one thing that means the most to you in life (sorry, kids).

There are stages associated with pickleball injuries that all players progress through on this journey. The first, of course, is denial. You aren't hurt, you're just sore. No treatment is needed, and you definitely aren't going to miss a match.

Over time, the denial stage gives way to the anger stage. The injury isn't getting better, and someone must be blamed.

"Why wasn't the match postponed when the court was clearly wet?"

"What kind of a doubles partner steps in front of me on that shot?"

"I never would have gotten hurt if we were given the standard warm-up time listed in the rule book."

It goes on and on. You are injured, and it's not your fault. Everyone in your path will feel your wrath in one way or another.

As your anger subsides, you shift into the bargaining phase. You begin to make deals — with yourself, of course — about how this injury will be managed.

"I'll skip practice tomorrow so I can play in the match on Wednesday."

"I'm going to practice today, but I won't run. I'll just work on volleys."

These deals do nothing to actually help you get healthy, and they are rarely upheld. That promise of "no running" is quickly broken, and you are soon sweating and limping your way back to the car.

Eventually, at long last, you arrive at the acceptance phase. You admit to yourself that this injury needs medical attention. You book an appointment with your physical therapist, and they aren't surprised in the least.

As you walk into the office for your appointment, the receptionist looks at you and asks plainly, "What did you hurt this time?"

# COMMON INJURIES FOR PICKLEBALL WEEKEND WARRIORS

You once thought that pickleball wouldn't expose you to injury.

Now that you know better, you are surprised to find just how many different injuries can stem from playing a game that looks like tennis was left in the dryer too long.

It seems that no part of the body is safe from damage on the pickleball battlefield. It starts with the Achilles tendon.

When you were young, you never thought about your Achilles tendon. It's back there, holding things together and keeping you moving, but never once was it a source of pain or even discomfort.

You are no longer young, however. And now, you are demanding that this tendon work overtime to help you lunge for a ball that is probably going to be out anyway.

Most of the time, you play through Achilles tendonitis with a combination of ibuprofen and sheer determination. Lingering in the back of your mind, however, is the threat of a complete rupture and more than a year of recovery.

Cold chills run down the back of your neck.

Lower back pain is another familiar partner for the die-hard dinker. Since this game is oddly tiny for some reason, much of it is played in a bent-over position. When was the last time you hit any shot other than a smash while actually standing upright? Exactly.

All that hunching does a number on your lumbar region. Getting out of bed in the morning has become a chore, and purchasing a $5,000 orthopedic mattress can't be far off.

## BROKEN AND PROUD

As the matches add up, you realize one thing about all of these injuries: You can play through most of them!

Being hurt doesn't have to stop you from keeping up with a relentless match and practice schedule. Sure, you walk through your daily life like a zombie extra in a bad movie, but who cares? You are still out there, racking up a few wins (and a lot more losses).

It turns out that pickleball isn't as safe as you expected. Injuries happen, and they can pile up fast.

Weirdly, they only make you love the game more. You feel like you are playing a real sport, even if the rest of the world might not see it the same way.

# COURT DRAMA AND PADDLE POLITICS

# 8

Think back to that very first game of pickleball. When you were invited to play, the premise was simple — enjoy a friendly, relaxed day out with friends.

No pressure. No competition. Just a casual game on a beautiful, sunny day.

This set the perception in your mind that pickleball is a friendly game. That first game was cordial, and you assumed it would always be that way.

Oh, how naïve you were.

## PICKLEBALL PEOPLE AREN'T SO NICE AFTER ALL

Everyone is friendly before the first ball is struck. The courts are filled with people who are all smiles and casual chatter. It's hard to imagine a more welcoming place than a pickleball court before the game begins.

Then everything changes.

Suddenly, you see a new side to these people — and it isn't pretty. The same person who just said they "love your paddle"

or are "obsessed with your shoes" is now staring you down over a disputed line call.

Not all the tension is directed at you. Sometimes, you're just an uncomfortable witness to a passionate argument between doubles partners who also happen to be married. Somehow, you get the sense that this argument is about more than just pickleball.

As the couple packs up and leaves silently after an 11–2 beating, one thing becomes crystal clear: These people mean business.

## THE PETTIEST ARGUMENTS IN SPORTS

Sports and arguments go hand in hand. For as long as humans have been playing games, they've been arguing about them.

But there's something uniquely petty about pickleball arguments. Maybe it's the fact that four adults are standing on a court not much bigger than a ping-pong table. Maybe it's the cheap plastic ball and matching t-shirts.

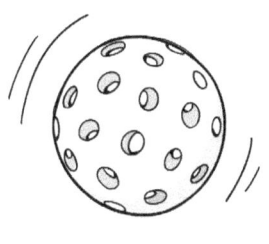

Whatever the case, when adults start getting riled up about a pickleball match, be sure to grab some popcorn — it's going to be good.

Line calls are at the heart of most disputes. Was it in or out? Such a simple question, and yet it can devolve into a full-on shouting match.

The best part is when players begin recreating the scene frame by frame: "Okay, I was standing here and you were over there. The ball came over this shoulder and I ducked. From my angle, I could *clearly* see it was out by an inch."

On and on it goes. It eventually gets settled — somehow — but no one walks away happy.

Serving is another minefield. The ball must be struck below the waist to be legal, but that's a fine line. Was it too high? Where was the paddle at contact?

Yes, these are real debates had by real adults — people with jobs, kids, responsibilities. Madness.

Then there are the scoring disputes — not about what happened during a point, but how many points each team has. That's right, arguments about counting.

Counting.

A skill mastered in kindergarten somehow turns into a rage-fest between four adults who can't manage to count to 11 without losing track.

Sometimes, you get dragged into these debates. More often, you watch others go off the rails and try to rope you in. "You saw it, right? That was clearly out."

## A HIERARCHY OF PICKLEBALL POWER

Like any human gathering, pickleball has a social structure. Everyone has their place, and rarely do people stray from their assigned roles. You *might* move up over time — but slowly. No one knows exactly how the system works, and no one dares question it. Rock the boat, and you might get tossed overboard.

At the top of the pyramid is the Alpha Paddle. This person runs the group — on and off the court. What they say goes. Period.

Those petty arguments we mentioned earlier? They don't happen in Alpha Paddle's games. They hold the final word on everything.

A step below is the Connector. This could be anyone, but let's be honest — it's usually a woman. Clipboard in hand, she organizes the whole operation and doesn't tolerate nonsense. She'll guide you once. If you mess up again, you're on your own.

And at the bottom are the Newbies. You were one, not long ago — wide-eyed and clueless. Some will rise. Others will fade away, eventually deciding to try something with lower stakes... like bowling.

# SCANDALS ON AND OFF THE COURT

It's one thing to argue about a serve. It's another thing entirely to get caught up in an actual scandal.

Some scandals stay on the court — like doubles partners suddenly splitting up mid-season. No one says why. Everyone speculates. Whispers abound.

But the real drama? Romantic entanglements.

Despite your best intentions to focus on the game, the gossip pulls you in. "His partner *used* to be his wife?" "How many partners has *that* guy had this year?" "Wait, *she's* playing mixed doubles with *him* now?"

It's a soap opera, and the plotlines are somehow *less* believable than actual TV.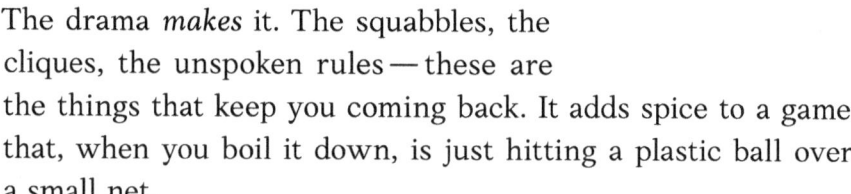

Is it all silly? Yes.

Do you want it to stop? Absolutely not.

The drama *makes* it. The squabbles, the cliques, the unspoken rules — these are the things that keep you coming back. It adds spice to a game that, when you boil it down, is just hitting a plastic ball over a small net.

Anything that makes that more entertaining? Bring it on.

# CHAPTER 9
# LETTING YOUR PICKLEBALL FREAK FLAG FLY

The embarrassment over playing pickleball didn't last long. Sure, you had said some nasty things before you tried it, but people forgot about that version of you pretty quickly.

Quickly, you settled into a comfortable middle ground. You weren't embarrassed about playing, but you didn't really shout about it, either. It was just a new hobby, and you talked about it with other players.

Not anymore.

These days, your pickleball freak flag flies high and you preach the gospel to anyone who will listen. In fact, it doesn't really matter if they are listening, because you are preaching anyway.

## THE STICKER LIFE

Stickers are so innocent. From a young age, you've probably used stickers to declare your love for particular people or things.

Maybe it was your favorite singer. Or an athlete. Or a vacation destination.

Whatever the case, stickers were an easy and cheap way to show the world what you were passionate about.

Nothing wrong with that. But pickleball players take it to another level. Like most things, the progression is slow and gradual at first, before it becomes a full-blown obsession.

At some point, you got a free water bottle at a tournament. It had the name of the event and the date, and it worked well. It became your favorite.

Fine. No problem there.

Then came the first sticker. It read, of course, "Please Dink Responsibly."

That's not the best pun, but it's not the worst. Whatever. If it stopped there, no one would even bat an eye.

It obviously doesn't stop there. The stickers just keep coming, with no end in sight.

Your laptop. Your car. Anything you own with a relatively flat surface is fair game.

No one in your life had any doubt that you were obsessed with pickleball, but now you are blasting it right in their faces and making it more apparent than ever that you have a passion. Or a problem.

# COMMITTING FASHION CRIMES

Pickleball gear looks great on the pickleball court.

It is purpose-built for the game, and the look lines up with what everyone else is wearing.

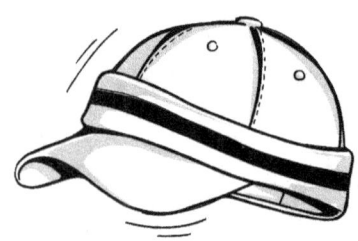

If the only place you ever wore your pickleball clothes and accessories was to the court, there would be no issue at all.

But that's not what you do, now is it?

Fashion crimes are a big part of flying your pickleball flag as proudly as possible. After all, you spent a lot of money on these items, so why shouldn't you use them as often as you can?

Soon enough, you are wearing court shoes to the grocery store. When you meet your friends for lunch, you pick out your "Dink or Die" tank top as the perfect look for the occasion.

It doesn't stop with clothes. You may also find yourself using your paddle bag for daily outings, even when no pickleball court will be anywhere in sight.

Even a date night with your spouse is not safe from the pickleball obsession. Despite having reservations at a nice restaurant, you come down the stairs wearing a "Parks and Rec Mixed Doubles Champion — Second Flight" t-shirt.

Your spouse would like to act surprised, but they aren't. They just look down, shake their head, and walk out to the car.

Not sure that you fall into this category in your pickleball evolution? Take the following simple test to find out.

Right now, go through the drawer in your dresser where you keep all of your t-shirts. How many of them are moisture-wicking? If that number is over 50%, congratulations, your pickleball freak flag is flying higher than most.

## A RECRUITING MISSIONARY

You are no longer satisfied just participating in pickleball. You now want to bring the rest of the world along with you.

As far as you are concerned, there are no strangers in a world where pickleball exists. There are only people who haven't yet been invited to an open play night.

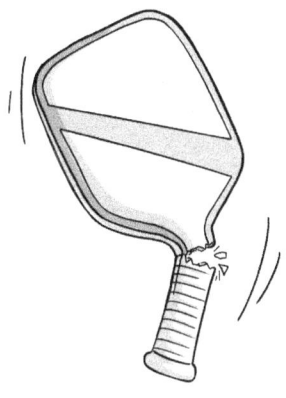

One of your favorite opportunities to recruit new players is when someone complains of a minor ache or pain. For example, when a co-worker says their shoulder is sore, you start extolling the virtues of pickleball to stay active and keep your body healthy.

Or, when the DoorDash driver is breathing hard after coming up your steps, you start talking about getting into a league to maintain a "base level of cardio."

All of those pickleball injuries we talked about earlier? Yeah, you conveniently forget to bring those up.

It's not just fitness that you use as a recruiting tool. You also talk about the social scene.

"You'll meet so many great new people!"

"League night is just like one big party!"

"I met my last two wives on the pickleball court!"

Whatever it takes. You just need to get your foot in the door and bring them out for a single match. As you know all too well, the rest will be history from there.

# MASTERING THE ART OF THE HUMBLE BRAG

As your skills grow in this silly game, it becomes harder and harder to keep your accomplishments to yourself.

Sure, you don't want to sound like you are bragging, but how can you keep this to yourself? How many people can say they finished in third place in the fourth division of the annual county pickleball competition?

Slowly, you develop your humble brag skills. You find a way to sneak things into conversations that highlight your abilities without being obvious about it (hint: It's still obvious).

The primary way you talk about your pickleball game with others (who didn't ask) is to sneak your rank into regular banter.

"Oh look, we parked in spot number four, almost as high as my pickleball rating!"

"I'll order the #3 special with fries, please. That's the only time I'm a 3, of course."

Each day is a new chance to squeeze your pickleball prowess into conversation.

It's also a nice move to correct people when they say that you "play" pickleball. Politely, but firmly, you inform them that you don't actually "play" pickleball — you compete in pickleball. There's a big difference.

A strange sense of ownership has taken over your relationship with pickleball. Despite being played by millions of people, you feel that this game is somehow "yours."

If pickleball comes up in conversation, you dive in and offer your authoritative opinion. It doesn't matter if you were asked, or even know the people who are talking. As an official (unofficial) representative of the pickleball community, your voice must be heard.

# BECOMING A LIFER

# 10

As the years pass, match points are won and lost and the injuries continue to pile up.

You haven't once contemplated quitting this game or even scaling back, but the fervor has faded. These days, you aren't so much obsessed with pickleball as you are one with the game.

It's as integral to daily life as breathing and eating, and you hardly even have to think about it anymore. You still love the game as much as you ever have, but now it's in a subtle, comfortable way.

## KEEPING IT TO YOURSELF

Where your pickleball personality was once marked by talking about the game as often as possible — with people who didn't ask — you are no longer so assertive about it.

Most of the bumper stickers have been taken off your car. When you get a new water bottle, you decide to keep it clean and free from your pickleball evangelism.

When you go to a party, you wear "normal" clothes. The "Dinkaholic" t-shirt stays in the closet more often than not.

You don't look back on the previous version of your pickleball self with regret, but you've changed. You've matured. Everyone in your life knows you take this game seriously, and that's enough.

The peace that has settled into this part of your life is welcome. It feels like you are right where you belong.

## THE QUIET ROUTINE OF THE COMMITTED

In many ways, the story arc of your relationship with pickleball mirrors the standard progression of a runner. New runners are famous for telling everyone in sight about how many miles they have logged.

As time passes, however, they keep those things to themselves and do all of that work in quiet solitude.

You are now much the same way with your pickleball life.

Do you play a lot? Of course.
Do you tell everyone about it?
Not really.

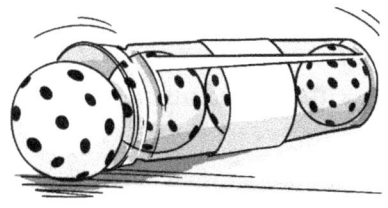

There is a standard rhythm and pace to your pickleball existence. Mondays and Wednesdays are league nights. Most Saturdays are reserved for tournaments.

In between, you fit in plenty of practice sessions. If anyone asks you to join a pick-up game, you are in. Everyone in the club knows where to find you, and knows you are always ready to join.

## CROSSING THE VOLUNTEER LINE

Volunteering always seemed like a boring way to spend time at a pickleball court.

Why just stand off to the side holding a clipboard when you could be out there on the court, your blistered fingers clinging to the worn grip on your paddle?

You didn't say it out loud, but volunteering was for old people.

Now you volunteer.

Just like when you first started playing this game, you didn't actually set out to be a volunteer. Someone asked, and you didn't have an excuse, so you said yes.

Quickly, you realized it wasn't so bad. It was actually a way to give your creaking joints a day off without having to stay away from the courts entirely.

It's not the same as playing, of course, but still better than nothing.

## GETTING THE KIDS INVOLVED— WHETHER THEY LIKE IT OR NOT

For the most part, you have given up on trying to drag people into this game with you.

If someone wants to learn, you are happy to help—but you are no longer the paddle-pusher that you were just a few short years ago.

Except with the kids. There's little more you want in life than to have your kids pick up a paddle and dink with the same passion that you do. Picturing it in your mind is enough to get your eyes a little watery.

Naturally, they aren't very interested. It's not that pickleball isn't a good game for kids. It is. The problem is you.

Anything that you do is naturally going to be seen as "uncool" in the eyes of your kids. That's just how nature works.

So, you turn to bribes.

"You can use the 'good' paddle if we go practice."

"I'll take you out for ice cream after we are done."

"We can ignore the rules and just hit the ball back and forth." (This one makes you cringe.)

So far, your efforts with the kids have gotten nowhere. They'll come along to play or watch every once in a while just to be nice, but they haven't been bitten by the bug yet.

You keep hoping. You remember how pickleball grabbed hold of you and wouldn't let go, and there will always be a part of you that hopes your kids catch the same condition.

## THE BODY OF A PICKLEBALLER

This game has changed your body. Sadly, that doesn't mean it has turned you into a shredded specimen of a human.

Rather, it has somehow built a specific type of strength while also wearing you down at the same time.

First, there are the tan lines. Your legs from the ankles up are golden and just a bit crispy. Below the sock line, however, is another story. You can't remember the last time your feet saw the light of day.

There is also the way you walk. It's not that you limp, necessarily. It's more that you *labor* as you move. Your stride gets you where you need to go, but it looks like a lot of work from the outside. And it feels like a lot of work from the inside.

There are tendons that have been overworked. Muscles that have been pulled, strained, and stretched. When your joints move, it sounds like someone is stepping on a bag of chips.

There are no illusions of getting your body "back into shape," because you aren't technically *out* of shape. You are just in pickleball shape, for better or worse.

## ACCEPTING YOUR LIFE SENTENCE

Even as your pickleball obsession was developing, you still considered taking up other hobbies.

Those dusty golf clubs in the garage called to you from time to time. Maybe you'd hit the driving range on a Sunday afternoon to loosen up your swing and contemplate a tee time with some buddies.

You also thought about mountain biking. Or woodworking. Or running. Or biking. And on and on.

These days, those thoughts are but a distant memory.

You've accepted that pickleball is it. This is your hobby, and that's the end of it.

There will be no golf comeback. You aren't going to buy a mountain bike, or do any running (beyond shuffling from the baseline to the net and back again).

This admission to yourself might sound like a defeat. It might sound like you are giving up on life. But it's actually quite the opposite. You've already found your life, and you don't need to keep searching.

Pickleball is the hobby you wanted and needed the whole time. And now that you have it, you'll simply be holding on and squeezing the life out of every last drop shot.

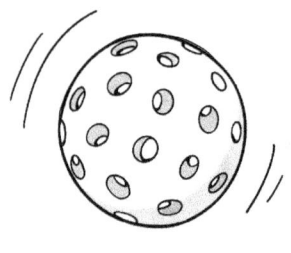

# CONCLUSION

It's been quite the journey.

From that awkward — but surprisingly enjoyable — first game, you have come a long way. You've won some matches, and even a couple of tournaments. You've lost plenty more. The experiences you've had in pickleball have taught you a lot about yourself, and continue to do so to this day.

You never knew you were so competitive. You didn't imagine that you'd be arguing with Becky from Accounts Payable about whether or not a small plastic ball landed on a line or beyond it.

Being so physically active has also permanently changed you physically — for better in some ways, and for worse in others.

Sports were never a big part of your life, and now a single sport is the biggest part of your life.

The physical activity and competition are great, but there is one thing that stands out as far and away the best thing about becoming an avid pickleballer: The people.

## A WONDERFUL BAND OF WEIRDOS

Without a doubt, your favorite part of the pickleball journey is the people you've met. The friends you've made. The experiences you've had with total strangers whom you would never have encountered any other way.

Sure, these people are odd. But so are you. It's a perfect fit.

After all, who else thinks it's fun to spend countless hours driving to play a tournament at 8 a.m. on a cold morning in a small town you've never heard of?

What sounds terrible to the average person sounds like heaven to a pickleballer.

These are your people, without a doubt.

## WRITING THE REST OF YOUR STORY

As we leave this book behind, the same can't be said for your pickleball journey.

That's still in progress—and there are still many more chapters to be added. You'll still lift a few more trophies. You'll definitely pick up a few more injuries.

And those arguments over line calls? Yeah, there will be more of those, too.

We hope you've enjoyed the book and that it's given you a chance to reflect on your journey so far. Stopping to appreciate where you've been is the best way to keep those memories alive and set new goals for the future.

So have fun out there. Keep dinking, keep sweating, and keep fighting for court position like your life depends on it.

Because in many ways, it does.

# LEAVE A REVIEW

If this book made you smile, laugh, or nod in guilty recognition—leave a quick review or star rating on Amazon.

It helps other "I'll-never-play" folks find the book… and admit they're hooked too.

Your paddle pals will thank you, and somewhere, a new player will hear that first magical "dink, dink, dink."

**To leave a review & help spread the word**

www.ingramcontent.com/pod-product-compliance
Lightning Source LLC
Chambersburg PA
CBHW071220070526
44584CB00019B/3089